AF394644

Britain's Best Gardens

written by
Kendra Wilson

Caisson Gardens (p.118)

Plas yn Rhiw (p.208)
Opposite: Great Dixter (p.68)

Charleston (p.88)

Contents

The Best For...

<table>
<tr><td>CONSERVATION</td><td>Many gardens listed here have biodiversity as the goal. This involves a spectrum of neatness, from the immaculately tended Caisson Gardens (p.118) at one end, to the volunteer-led Eden Nature Garden (p.48) at the other.</td></tr>
<tr><td>TEA & CAKE</td><td>Cake goes hand in hand with garden visiting – and Coton Manor excels at this (p.154) – but a good lunch is also welcome. Iford Manor (p.130) is justly proud of its cafe and bakery, well situated for estate walks. Have tea on the lawn overlooking the bay at Plas yn Rhiw (p.208) and be sure to try the Battenberg cake.</td></tr>
<tr><td>PLANT SHOPPING</td><td>For choice and quality, a plant nursery beats a garden centre, and it makes sense to shop in the garden you've just been admiring. Unusual home-grown plants are guaranteed at Great Dixter (p.68). Don't miss Surreal Succulents when visiting Tremenheere Sculpture Gardens (p.144).</td></tr>
<tr><td>VISITING WITH KIDS</td><td>Lullingstone Castle (p.86) is run by people who are young at heart, and children can roam free at this unpretentious ancestral hall. Of the many themed events, look out for the Plant Hunter's Weekend, with tour guides dressed in character. Cotswold Wildlife Park (p.60) is similarly un-bossy and appealing in its eccentricity.</td></tr>
<tr><td>A KITCHEN GARDEN</td><td>Overlooked by the village church, the walled gardens at Rousham (p.64) burst with flowers and produce, and are a pleasant surprise after the formal garden's grandeur; meanwhile, Waltham Place (p.80) offers an insight into biodynamic gardening.</td></tr>
</table>

Many of the gardens listed here are in designated Areas of
Outstanding Natural Beauty, or just in beautiful places. If you
are passing through out of season, check the website; there is
excellent walking at Doddington (p.172), Iford (p.130),
Mapperton (p.112), Lowther Castle (p.174) and Chatsworth
(p.186), to name a few.

Gone are the days when gardens went quiet in August because
their aristocratic owners were shooting in Scotland; they are
planted for year-round enjoyment. Dutch plantsman Piet Oudolf
must take part of the credit for this; explore his 21st-century
gardens at Hauser & Wirth (p.114) and Pensthorpe (p.108). At
more historic locations, like Hidcote (p.158) and Sissinghurst
(p.54), winter is an excellent time to see a garden's 'bones',

Don't allow the calming effects of a garden visit to evaporate in
traffic afterwards; many gardens are easily accessed without a
car. Let a bus do the climbing up to Highgate Village and take
time to explore OmVed (p.26), with views over London.
Tremenheere (p.144) is accessible by train from Paddington;
hop off at Penzance and take a bus or walk a pleasant two miles.
Other train and walk combos are Lullingstone (p.86) (alight
at Eynsford) and Dilston (p.198) (Corbridge).

Garden memoirs can be a surprisingly fun read; Vita Sackville-
West's *In Your Garden* shows the writer at her most engaging,
and her son Nigel Nicolson's frank biography *Portrait of a
Marriage* is a riveting insight into life at Sissinghurst (p.54).
Christopher Lloyd of Great Dixter (p.68) was delightfully
opinionated in all his books; *The Well-Tempered Garden* is the
classic. Derek Jarman's wide-ranging notes are humorous and
poignant, while sharing real garden knowledge. *Derek Jarman's
Garden* has wonderful photographs of Prospect Cottage
(p.78) by his friend Howard Sooley.

A new leaf for British gardens

The UK has long been described as 'a nation of gardeners', but it's an old-fashioned image, evoking grandparents tending runner beans and country squires opening their gates for charity. Now, the idea of a gardening nation is gaining new resonance, with people of all ages and backgrounds unabashedly growing food and flowers. And garden visiting is only getting better. The gardens in this guide are as likely to be found on a sliver of wasteland or a former car park as an ancestral estate that has been managed since Domesday. None of them are boring. They all have this in common: they are stewarded by people who care about the landscape and are keen to share ideas with nature-curious visitors. Some have children's amusement firmly up front; others do not.

For some people, the intrigue of a place lies in its saga of neglect and restoration. The interiors at William Morris's Kelmscott (p.50) add to the garden experience, and so can a tour. Your level of engagement is up to you, but all the gardens included here have stories to tell, and their beauty lies in the self-expression of gardeners past and present. It seems that secret gardens and reimagined ruins are the ones we love best, and it follows that the most interesting British gardens are not over-explained.

The spectacular locations of many of the entries in this book make it clear why people have gardened in them for millennia. The British Isles are uniquely blessed with a (historically) temperate situation: not too dry, not too hot and not too cold. Clearly this is no longer a permanent guarantee, but our climate sheds light on the affinity that Brits have long had for plant-collecting; species from faraway places get on well here. Colonialism is one aspect of this acquisitiveness, but you can also look at it this way: people who love plants are interested in conservation, and the specimens that are carefully maintained here form a kind of ark in an uncertain world.

Traditionally, formal gardens were arranged for their owners' pleasure; power came into it, and showing off. The new ethos is more interesting; OmVed (p.26) in north London is a Community Interest Company, operating for the benefit of its users rather than for private profit. Gardening now is intensely connected with boosting biodiversity; it gives us some measure of autonomy in our own patch. At the same time, privately owned gardens have intensified their appeal, with good food, stays, walks and workshops. Iford Manor (p.130) has all of these; the owners describe it as a sanctuary for 'aesthetes, nature and food lovers' – more engaging than simply 'historic house and garden'

Many of the gardens here are small or free or open year-round. Others have walks that are permanently accessible. Check individual websites for openings; when we say that a place is open over several months in a season, it doesn't mean that it's open every day. Also seek out the National Garden Scheme for garden openings near you, and see what grows well in your area. By looking, we become better gardeners.

Kendra Wilson
Oxford, 2026

Chelsea Physic Garden

London's oldest botanic garden

It is worth travelling to this secluded 4-acre garden by public transport, then walking through the neighbouring streets to get a sense of its river-facing atmosphere. Before the Chelsea Embankment was built to accommodate the Victorian sewer system (and traffic), the Thames was a more reliable thoroughfare than roads, and it lapped up to the edge of the Physic Garden. Apothecaries were able to go herb hunting with ease downstream and, on a grander scale, receive and exchange plants and seeds from around the world. Established in 1673, the Physic Garden can claim many firsts – the earliest heated greenhouse (1680), the first purpose-built rockery for growing plants, the first forced rhubarb (a happy accident), and so on. Its many special attributes include its small and charming glasshouses and utilitarian layout; it is a place of learning with a particular slant on medicinal and useful plants, and its intentions have never been decorative.

66 Royal Hospital Road, London, SW3 4HS
Open year-round
Paid entry
chelseaphysicgarden.co.uk

Barbican Estate

Brutalism meets its match

It's easy to get lost at the Barbican Estate, but make time to seek out Beech Gardens (on John Trundle Highwalk, opposite Barbican Tube Station) and the Conservatory, undergoing a revamp by garden design practice Harris Bugg Studio. The quality of greenery at this densely inhabited urban village and arts complex has generally taken second place to the showstopping Brutalist architecture, but during the more recent re-waterproofing of Beech Gardens – essentially a roof garden – it was decided that the high-maintenance, traditional planting could be improved upon. Urban horticulture expert Nigel Dunnett was called in, comparing the windswept site – hot and dry in summer, cold in winter – to the steppes of Eurasia, able to support grassland species and small trees. The visual success of the horticulture here is that it doesn't attempt to compete with the permanent hard landscape. Our attention is pulled into the planting; resilient grasses and euphorbias are cheered by garden-sized multi-stem trees, and a mix of reassuringly familiar alliums, poppies and salvias.

Silk Street, London, EC2Y 8DS
Open year-round
Free to visit
barbican.org.uk

The Garden Museum

Make a detour for this cosmopolitan display

As a niche destination, the Garden Museum punches way above its weight; the restaurant alone is worth crossing town for. The shaded entrance garden, free to passers-by, was designed as a buffer between this former church of St Mary and the traffic of Lambeth Bridge. Inside, the museum has an urbane air, incorporating gravestones into smooth floors and tombs of notable locals into what is now an enclosed courtyard garden. The garden, redesigned in 2017 by Dan Pearson Studio, is a cabinet of curiosities; home to rare plant specimens and honouring plant hunters past and present. A 17th-century tomb splendidly carved with landscapes, shells and exotic animals, was made for the royal gardeners John Tradescant the Elder and John the Younger, who introduced some key plants and trees to England (such as lilac, horse chestnut and tulip tree). Just across the road, the Garden Museum's new community garden is accessible to all.

Lambeth Palace Road, London, SE1 7LB
Open year-round
Paid entry
gardenmuseum.org.uk

Kew Gardens

Country in the city

For anyone who can remember when Kew Gardens charged a penny for entry, its current prices will come as a shock. Booking ahead is cheaper and looking at a map first is wise; there is a lot to cover. With truly vast Victorian glasshouses and the smallest royal palace in the land, Kew is also a leading scientific institution. The Millennium Seed Bank (in Wakehurst) aims to conserve botanic diversity; the horticultural forensics department aids police work. Perhaps you just want to look at plants: a winter stroll will present not just one good-looking holly, but a whole collection – useful for window shopping. Beautifully realised set pieces lead visitors to unusual vantage points, such as on the Treetop Walkway or the middle of the lake via the minimalist bridge. Find some *rus in urbe* at Queen Charlotte's Cottage, set deep within a curated forest (in other words, the Arboretum) where trees meet the River Thames. Kew has great style, attracting children and adults to the same things.

Richmond, TW9 3AE
Open year-round
Paid entry
kew.org/kew-gardens

OmVed Gardens

Beautiful and useful community garden

Hidden down an alley in Highgate Village, OmVed is itself a kind of village: a 3-acre garden, with a group of charming, steep-roofed wooden buildings at its core. Variously designed for seed saving, cooking, teaching and growing, the structures reflect OmVed's interest in interconnectedness, and our place in the world. Gardened regeneratively and developed from tarmacked wasteland by the landscape designer Paul Gazerwitz, this community space offers elegant design ideas at every turn. Look out for the permeable paving around chic compost bins, unusual edible plants spilling from walls made from a better class of cinderblock and circles of Corten steel, submerged in the kitchen garden forming raised beds. With ponds replacing a car park at the bottom of the sloping site, rainwater has been given a destination. An absence of cars adds to the sense of enchantment; visitors book ahead for events at different price levels (and a free art exhibition in summer). The views over London are spectacular; take in Highgate cemetery's gothic splendour just down the hill.

1 Townsend Yard, London, N6 5JF
Open year-round
Mix of free and paid events
omvedgardens.com

Inner Temple Garden

Leafy seclusion in the City

To an outsider, London's Inns of Court have an air of mystery, and the same can be said for their gardens. Entry to the Inner Temple Garden is through a discreet doorway on Fleet Street, leading past the 12th-century Temple Church to the official garden entrance at Crown Office Row. Between here and the River Thames are three hidden acres of sloping, horticultural theatre, mainly enjoyed by the lawyers who work here. At the top, the wildly exuberant High Border screens a car park and sets the scene: colourful perennials mix with towering exotics by the buildings and walls, while the lawn boasts deckchairs as well as shaggy meadow grass (with haystacks in late summer) that spreads out from venerable London plane trees. Restricted opening hours add to the secretive atmosphere; this is a lunchtime park (open 12:30–3pm), with no obvious point of entry to passersby on the Embankment. Plan ahead and allow yourself longer than an hour.

Inner Temple, London, EC4Y 7HL
Open year-round
Free to visit
innertemple.org.uk/estate-garden/
the-inner-temple-garden

Horniman Museum Gardens

Engagingly instructive displays

When Frederick Horniman, MP, left his eponymous museum to Londoners in 1901, it was intended that the park-like gardens would do their share as places of 'instruction and enjoyment'. They achieve this; there are signs everywhere, and you'll find yourself wanting to read them all. Traditional garden set pieces are rethought: the pond in the Sunken Garden was deepened to support more biodiversity, and elsewhere beds overflow with intensely coloured flowers and vegetables used for dyeing (all charmingly explained). The Grasslands Garden, developed by horticultural ecologist James Hitchmough with Horniman's gardeners, is cleverly designed to show distinct prairie grasslands from North America and South Africa. Along the park's perimeter, a broad range of closely planted trees and shrubs demystifies the concept of 'micro-forests': absorbing noise and fumes from the road, they provide habitat, store carbon, mitigate flooding and add layers of leaf colour to the scene. Take a notebook and a camera.

100 London Road, London, SE23 3PQ

Open year-round

Free to visit

horniman.ac.uk

Covent Garden Playground & Gardens

Urban children's play space reimagined

Tucked away from the hubbub of Covent Garden Piazza on Drury Lane, this is a quiet public space with a few surprises. Formerly an overspill graveyard to St Martin-in-the-Fields, it was locked up and overgrown until the 19th century, when the Victorian social reformer (and founder of the National Trust) Octavia Hill campaigned to open it as a small children's park. The playground persists, but it's also a fascinating garden, with planting that is more rarefied than civic. This is due to a collaboration with the avant-garde Swedish nurseryman Peter Korn, who brought all the plant material over in his car (to avoid wasteful packaging). Korn specialises in growing a diverse range of plants in sand and gravel – further minimising wastage, since the old, exhausted soil is simply covered over. Plants that are chosen for their drought tolerance grow strong and, in this lean environment, weeds are easily removed. As a study in plant resilience (and beauty) in tough urban conditions, it's a must-see. Children like it, too.

57 Drury Lane, London, WC2B 5SN
Open year-round
Free to visit
instagram.com/coventgardenplayground

The Regent's Park

The jewel in the crown of London's Royal Parks

Commissioned by the Prince Regent in the 1810s, the eponymous park's 410 acres comprise the most stylish of central London's Royal Parks. John Nash designed the site, as well as the surrounding neighbourhood, giving the whole a sense of occasion – even without the Regency zoo and outdoor theatre. Near the entrance at Chester Gate, the Avenue Gardens pair formality with gleeful flamboyance, and the rose display at Queen Mary's Gardens rises above the genre. Instead of the usual shrubbery, 12,000 roses are surrounded by a delightful Mediterranean garden, leading the visitor along winding paths in sun and shade, amid an inspiring and vast array of low-water planting. Avoiding crowds is easy at the Regent's Park, and never more so than at St John's Lodge to the north of the Inner Circle, often described as a 'secret garden'. The latest attraction, a garden to honour Queen Elizabeth II, is built on former brownfield; plants grow in gravelly sand, and the focus is on resilience.

London, NW1 4NR

Open year-round

Free to visit

royalparks.org.uk/visit/parks/regents-park-primrose-hill

The Exchange

Destination garden in south-east London

The Old Library in Erith and its newer garden have much in common: created a century apart, they are both community spaces, built to the highest standard. The Scottish-American philanthropist Andrew Carnegie (of Carnegie Hall in New York) built the library on the proviso that future funding and maintenance would be from local people. Having lost direction by 2016, the library was taken on and restored as a community resource by some enterprising residents, who ambitiously approached top landscape designer Sarah Price to make a garden. The result is a palette of silvery green shrubs and trees, plus flowers of resonant colours, all planted by volunteers, creating a serene atmosphere despite the very nearby roads. More mature plants were donated by the fashion house Hermès, after a collaboration with Price, and its pathways of herringbone brick and aggregate were made at community workshops held by landscape practice Local Works Studio using recycled building waste.

The Old Library, Walnut Tree Road, Erith, DA8 1RA
Open year-round
Free to visit
theexchangeerith.com/the-garden

Eden Nature Garden

Churchyard haven for wildlife

As a place to sit down, wander, volunteer, learn about biodiversity or all of the above, Eden Nature Garden in Clapham is an exemplary public space. But that doesn't mean that it's preachy: signs discreetly explain the cycle of life, but it's the garden itself that has the most to say. Stewarded by the serendipitously named Benny Hawksbee (right), even the shed is put to work, supporting myriad habitats for solitary bees. Holes drilled into wood, hollow stems gathered together in an orderly way and nesting boxes packed with sand provide vital homes for more than 20 different wild bee species. Tucked into a slice of church land, the narrow garden is separated from St Paul's Churchyard by a path that connects the stillness of Rectory Grove with the traffic of Wandsworth Road. Expect to find a mini meadow, a woodland area, small pond and peaceful coexistence between people and local wildlife.

St Paul's Church, Rectory Grove, London, SW4 0DZ
Open year-round
Free to visit
edennaturegarden.org

Kelmscott Manor

William Morris's rural inspiration

'The garden is quite unaffected and very pleasant,' wrote William Morris, the 19th-century designer, manufacturer and social agitator on first seeing the small Elizabethan manor of Kelmscott. Sitting amid water meadows on a tributary of the Thames, it was his weekend bolthole and inspiration; a place to look away from Victorian England towards a dream of quieter times. This is still the appeal: both house and garden remain largely as they were, with the recent reintroduction of Morris & Co furniture and hand-blocked wallpaper and textiles enlivening the space once again. The pleasingly simple garden was restored in the 1960s, with local varieties of fruit trees that would have been available during Morris's tenure. The gnarled mulberry tree gives shelter to British spring ephemerals, including wild tulips, which lay dormant during the neat lawn decades, but have since been allowed to sing in a manner that Morris would surely have enjoyed.

Lechlade, GL7 3HJ
Open April–October
Paid entry
kelmscottmanor.org.uk

Sissinghurst

The famous creation of Vita Sackville-West

Harold Nicolson, the husband of Vita Sackville-West – gardener, writer and uncloseted lesbian – described the garden they made at Sissinghurst as 'a series of escapes from the world'. Not a grand house, but a hodgepodge of castle ruins, with living quarters dotted around the garden that is itself a collection of rooms. The White Garden was inspired by the barn owl that would fly through as the couple sat down to dinner outside; the flame-hued Sunset Garden was where they'd spend the late afternoon. Harold made sense of the site by drawing out walks and paths with a ruler, while Vita blurred the lines with old roses and 'wildlings': plants that blew in from beyond the garden perimeter. The humanity of this joint enterprise (where Vita maintained the upper hand) has survived its immense fame. The National Trust property is maintained along organic principles, and the respected head gardener, Troy Scott Smith, has been able to let it evolve and relax. 'Sissinghurst is breathing again,' says a past gardener.

Biddenden Road, near Cranbrook, TN17 2AB
Open year-round
Paid entry
nationaltrust.org.uk/visit/kent/sissinghurst-castle-garden

Cotswold Wildlife Park & Gardens

Delight in the unexpected

Two miles outside the Cotswold town of Burford sits one of the area's many favoured houses, this one a Georgian-Gothic gem in its own park. The reindeer to the left of the entrance gate seem almost normal in the setting, while ostriches to the right do not. Stately trees are dotted around and, on the front lawn, a herd of grazing rhino. There is an appreciation of gardening at this family-run zoological collection; the spirited planting is intended to bring cheer to animals and people alike. Meerkats look out on a dramatic staging of cacti and succulents in an island bed, and Kniphofia (red hot pokers) from South Africa mix with jewel-coloured salvias from South America, among North American prairie flowers where the rhino roam. Calmly instructive (giant bamboo is the staple diet of bamboo lemurs and helps to feed the population here), the gardens also embrace high Victoriana, displaying 10,000 bedding plants (grown from seed), and the brightest tulips grouped around hardy palm trees.

Bradwell Grove, Burford, OX18 4JP

Open year-round

Paid entry

cotswoldwildlifepark.co.uk

Rousham House & Gardens

William Kent's quiet masterpiece

Ask a garden designer to name their favourite garden in England, and chances are it'll be Rousham. It is a transcending garden visit on many levels. The sense of a parallel universe begins before you reach the entrance; languorous longhorn cattle are a part of the pastoral landscape that is ever-present within the garden's 25 acres. Cared for by the same family that built the house in the 1630s, a notice states that there is no tea room, nor entry to under-15s. The effect is to keep attention focused on the garden and views over the landscape. There is drama at the end of the bowling green, where a lion eats a horse in stone, and mystery in the designed woodland below, with Antinous – the lover of the Emperor Hadrian – standing in a pool of light amid trees. The garden is the masterpiece of English architect William Kent, whose classical structures and subtle placing of sculptures were informed by a decade in Italy. Picnics are permitted in this predominantly green landscape; tucked away by the house, a walled garden bursts with colour.

Bicester, OX25 4QU

Open year-round

Paid entry

rousham.org

Great Dixter

Legendary Arts and Crafts garden

It's probably the most respected garden in the British Isles, due in no small part to the head gardener and CEO Fergus Garrett. Formerly the protégé of the iconoclastic gardener and writer Christopher Lloyd, who lived at Great Dixter all his life, Garrett has taken something great and made it greater. Now run as a charitable trust, it is a magnet for horticulturalists; a historic Arts and Crafts garden that never stands still. By the medieval front porch, seasonal flowers jostle with eccentric evergreens in pots of every size – a taster for the highly tuned plantsmanship in the famous Long Border, the Sunk Garden and the Peacock Garden. Go for the spring meadows or seek coolness in high summer under the canopy of the enclosed Exotic Garden: once a formal rose garden, it's a distillation of the experimental and exuberant approach of this charming place.

Northiam, Rye, TN31 6PH
Open April–October
Paid entry
greatdixter.co.uk

Magdalen College Gardens

Oxford grandeur, accessible to all

The breathtakingly beautiful city of Oxford is blessed with generous quantities of green space and flowing water. There are also many high walls and closed doors, but Magdalen College, one of the oldest and grandest, welcomes paying visitors to its 100 acres of grounds behind the High Street. With highlights including Addison's Walk, a treelined path around an island water meadow featuring a rare display of blooming snake's head fritillaries in spring; an 18th-century deer park; a wisteria-clad, 15th-century cloistered quad; ancient trees; immaculate lawns and herbaceous borders, it's well worth the nominal fee. The Oxford Botanic Garden, the oldest in the UK, is just across the road; beyond that is the un-ticketed Christ Church Meadow, with walks that take in views of longhorn cattle, boat practice and abundant roses at Merton College, tumbling over the walls on Deadman's Walk.

Oxford, OX1 4AU
Open year-round
Paid entry
magd.ox.ac.uk/visiting-magdalen-college

Benton End

The dream that came true

Until recently, the artist–gardener Cedric Morris was chiefly known in plant circles as a breeder of refined irises in antique colours – many of them lost. People recalled his magical garden, next to the radical mid-century art school that he ran from his Suffolk manor house with his partner, Arthur Lett-Haines (pupils included Lucian Freud and Maggi Hambling). This had also been lost. Then, in a kind of miracle, Benton End was majority gifted to the Garden Museum in 2021, with a request that it should be a place of creativity once again. A careful restoration has allowed the garden to reveal its secrets, with bulbs and perennials that Morris collected on his travels around the Mediterranean and North Africa reappearing in the garden, along with reintroductions from the friends and protégés who have kept the Morris flame alive by nurturing the plants he gave away. New landscaping comes from Sarah Price, an artist–gardener herself. Pre-book tickets via the Garden Museum.

Benton Street, Hadleigh, Suffolk, IP7 5JR
Opening summer 2026
Paid entry
gardenmuseum.org.uk/benton-end

Prospect Cottage

Derek Jarman's free-spirited shingle garden

The garden at Prospect Cottage is inseparable from its location at Dungeness, a desolate headland of shingle on the Kent coast that is owned by a private estate, and largely free of fences. The plot spreads towards the horizon; find somewhere to park (preferably not in front of the house) and immerse yourself in a different kind of cottage garden, made by the artist and writer Derek Jarman decades ago. Jarman's posthumous book, *Derek Jarman's Garden*, is worth reading before you go; he entertainingly records making island beds out of large pebbles (jutting upwards like dragons' teeth) to elevate Dungeness natives such as sea kale and horned poppy, to which he added plants from all over that would respond well to the searing sun and fierce, salty wind. The garden is now tended by skilled horticulturalists and is more elegant, contrasting nicely with the decommissioned nuclear power station as a backdrop and, ideally, a setting sun.

Dungeness Road, Romney Marsh, TN29 9NE
Open year-round
Free to visit
creativefolkestone.org.uk/prospect-cottage

Waltham Place

Elegance and ecology combined

Waltham Place is notably anonymous, with a 'no photos' policy and an entrance that is easy to miss. Inside is a truly unique garden: the layout is historically formal but the plants are not – they sprout where they have seeded, and persistent weeds are tolerated as groundcover. The effect is remarkably aspirational. Having gained organic status even before the King at Highgrove, the estate's occupants (whose family bought it in 1910) have long been forward-thinking. Back in 2000, the current owner, Strilli Oppenheimer, made the prescient decision to hire the late Dutch plantsman Henk Gerritsen to make the gardens more 'wild and fuzzy'. Ornamental plants are assessed for their value to insects and other creatures and are allowed to express themselves, growing and self-seeding naturally. Framed by immaculately clipped hedges, both bumpy and straight, Gerritsen's way with design is at its most glorious in a yew-lined double border of perennials and grasses, given rhythm by semi-circles of beech. The estate is biodynamic; join the queue for raw milk at the farm shop.

Church Hill, White Waltham, SL6 3JH
Open June–September
Paid entry
walthamplace.com

Balmoral Cottage

For people in the know

An easy way to see private gardens is through the National Garden Scheme, which raises money for health charities. Charlotte Molesworth's Balmoral Cottage garden is not generally open, but the NGS will get you there. Developed over 40 years with her husband Donald, this is an artist's garden, evident in the lovely reuse of found materials and the extraordinary bravura of her topiary. Evergreens of all kinds are clipped into wave-topped walls, animals and tall chess pieces, more beautiful than eccentric. Each green sculpture has been grown from cuttings, with yew a favourite; Molesworth will take a five-year-old specimen, cut a waist into the middle, and see what ideas it offers up. Hidden down a track that leads off Benenden's village green, the cottage is almost halfway between Sissinghurst (p.54) and Great Dixter (p.68). Plan a garden visit around one of Molesworth's openings and discover why this topiary garden is an insider's favourite. Alternatively, visit for the open garden-studio weekend in August.

The Green, Benenden, TN17 4DL
Open select days only
Paid entry
ngs.org.uk/gardens/balmoral-cottage-tn1

The World Garden, Lullingstone Castle

Travel the globe in a walled garden

The same family has been at Lullingstone Castle since 1361, and gardening has been a serious interest for the last few generations. Which is why Tom Hart Dyke, young heir to the estate, was plant hunting in South America in 2000, and decided to go that bit further into the Colombian jungle to find some orchids – at which point he was kidnapped by guerrilla militants. Told by his captors to prepare to die, he spent what he believed would be his final hours sketching a dream garden containing plants from across the globe, laid out according to their native countries. When Hart Dyke's life was spared and he returned home after a nine-month ordeal, he set about planting the 'world' in Lullingstone's 18th-century walled garden. The result is charming and educational in equal measure: even if your knowledge of plants is limited to a small palette of likes and dislikes, it would be hard not to rethink pampas grass after seeing it growing in 'South America' alongside ever-chic purple top Verbena. The garden is imbued with a spirit of 'live life as though each day is your last'.

Dartford, DA4 0JA

Open year-round

Paid entry

lullingstonecastle.co.uk

Charleston

Bloomsbury in the country

Charleston is located on a working farm, which is why Vanessa Bell, her lover Duncan Grant and his lover, Bunny Garnett, rented it in 1916. Several members of the Bloomsbury Group were conscientious objectors, and farm work was one way to avoid the draft. The house and its walled kitchen garden became a sanctuary and a gathering place for their friends. A house tour with an impassioned guide enhances the experience of what is essentially a very lovely cottage garden beyond the French windows. Impressions of interior decoration mixed with tales of complex domestic arrangements flow outside, where apple trees tangle with roses amid aromatic herbs and flowers. It was a place to paint and a subject for painting; when the frescoed house interior was saved from whitewash in the '80s, Bell and Grant's flower paintings were used as a reference in restoring the garden. Be sure to visit Monk's House, a 20-minute drive away – the home of Bell's non-gardening sister, Virginia Woolf, and Woolf's gardening husband, Leonard.

Firle, BN8 6LL
Open year-round
Paid entry
charleston.org.uk

Ventnor Botanic Garden

Continent-facing microclimate for plants

Here's an Isle of Wight garden with a difference. Not only is Ventnor Botanic Garden refreshingly *un*manicured, it's also home to a National Collection of Puya, nicknamed the 'sheep-eating plant' for the way it traps animals in its spiky leaves so that they starve and die at its base (their decomposing bodies acting as fertiliser). Located at the southern tip of the island, Ventnor has a welcoming microclimate for plants that wouldn't stand a chance on the British mainland, including garden favourites such as red hot pokers from South Africa. Because of the warmer climate, the fate of plants in these conditions is also a way of researching future gardening in the face of climate change. Visitors can explore 22 acres representing different geographic zones with compatible climates (such as the Andes, for Puya). Plants are grown in naturalistic communities rather than being clearly labelled; in a garden that aims to be carbon-neutral, a relaxed appearance is the way forward.

Undercliff Drive, Ventnor, Isle of Wight, PO38 1UL

Open year-round

Paid entry

botanic.co.uk

Cambridge Botanic Garden

Beauty in botany

There is an energy about the botanic garden in Cambridge that may be a result of its relative youth, having been at the current site since 'only' 1846. Half a mile from the train station, it was moved from a smaller central location to reflect the enthusiasms of the then Professor of Botany, John Stevens Henslow. Under his benign guidance, botany became one of the university's most popular subjects, in close engagement with the volume of new plant discoveries at that time. Instead of a physic garden ('a drug plant nursery for medical students', in the words of the CBG), the new site was for the experimental study of plants, with an emphasis on the variation of species within plant families – ideas that were famously developed by Henslow's pupil, Charles Darwin. This is brilliantly brought to life along the Main Walk, with pairings of same-but-different conifer trees, now splendidly mature. The glasshouses, too, are in a class of their own.

1 Brookside, Cambridge, CB2 1JE

Open year-round

Paid entry

botanic.cam.ac.uk

Newnham College Gardens

Warm-hearted college garden with public access

Separated from the hustle of Cambridge by the River Cam, Newnham sits down a tree-lined avenue. Mention to the porter that you are here for the gardens, and you will be waved through at no charge. Framed by graceful buildings of red brick, 'curved like ships' windows' (as described by Virginia Woolf in *A Room of One's Own*), the 17-acre gardens are somehow self-effacing while rising to the occasion. Past the sunken garden of roses and lavender, and beyond the lawns, there are nooks aplenty for contemplation and country trees mingle with spring bulbs in rough grass. Along the Nut Walk, blue-bells and other wildflowers thrive in the dappled shade. British landscape designer Gertrude Jekyll's thumbprint is felt in the lively herbaceous borders (the only part of her 1911 plan to be used), and near the tennis courts there is a growing iris collection. The pigs and chickens once kept here are gone, but an orchard and student allotments persist, continuing to offer the 'fresh air, exercise and wholesome food' that was proposed by Newnham's first Principal in the late 19th century.

Sidgwick Avenue, Cambridge, CB3 9DF

Open year-round

Free to visit

newn.cam.ac.uk/about/gardens

Houghton Hall & Gardens

Stately garden with permanent outdoor art collection

With its immaculate Palladian exterior, the hall at Houghton still inspires awe in the way that its creator, Sir Robert Walpole (Britain's first prime minister and a noted tastemaker), intended. There isn't a garden on immediate view, but a deer park, with insouciant white fallow deer wandering past the house facade. They are separated from the building by a ha-ha (a deep, reinforced ditch that livestock cannot cross). The 1720s landscape remains elegantly uncluttered, despite a permanent outdoor art collection, including pieces by Richard Long and Antony Gormley. Formality is loosened in the 5-acre walled garden, designed by Isabel and Julian Bannerman. Divided into separate, yew-hedged enclosures, it is a mood board of garden history, with swirling flower beds, arches of fruit, flowery English borders and a rustic temple, its pediment stuffed with antlers from the park.

King's Lynn, PE31 6TY
Open May–September
Paid entry
houghtonhall.com

The Manor at Hemingford Grey

Atmospheric setting for the Green Knowe books

It feels like almost too much to ask: the possibility of a garden with personality, history *and* good planting – yet no crowds. The Manor at Hemingford Grey is such a place. Its character is so palpable, it feels haunted. The garden's creator, author Lucy M. Boston, moved here on the eve of World War II and later used it as the fictionalised setting for her much-loved series of children's books, *Green Knowe*. History: it's one of the oldest continuously inhabited houses in the UK, dating from the 1130s. Now overseen by Lucy's daughter-in-law, Diana Boston – whose late husband illustrated the *Green Knowe* books – the garden is fabulously romantic, with elevated cottage garden plants relaxing between well-turned topiary and a moat. It's a watery site: leave your car in the village and enter through the garden gate via the banks of the Great Ouse. A tour of the atmospheric house can be arranged in advance.

Hemingford Grey, Huntingdon, PE28 9BN
Open year-round
Paid entry
greenknowe.co.uk

Pensthorpe

Sculpted gardens and pioneering conservation

It took a farmer with a love of wading birds and wildfowl to create this wetland of lakes and ponds out of his gravelly acres. Being a keen gardener as well as bird appreciator, Bill Makins took a chance on then little-known Piet Oudolf, giving the Dutch nurseryman his first public commission in the UK: designing and planting a garden to celebrate the Millennium. Signature groupings of perennials that look as lovely in winter as they do in summer merge gracefully into the wider reclaimed landscape. The original ethos has continued as the reserve has expanded under the ownership of Deb and Bill Jordan (the cereal people). A curving boardwalk crosses a recreated native wildflower meadow beside the River Wensum; the Wildlife Habitat Garden attracts specific animals with its designated bat and moth wall, and bee and butterfly banks. Children will love Pensthorpe's adventure playground, which balances wood, metal and tastefulness with a daredevil experience, while the new cafe incorporates the remnants of a 16th-century church.

Pensthorpe, Fakenham, NR21 0LN
Open year-round
Paid entry
pensthorpe.com

Mapperton

A dream of Dorset

For Thomas Hardy fans, the West Dorset countryside delivers; it's intensely atmospheric. Mapperton is two miles from the town of Beaminster (Emminster in *Tess of the D'Urbervilles*) and within easy reach of the fossil-laden Jurassic cliffs. The coastline is a World Heritage Site; the house and garden are cradled in an Area of Outstanding Natural Beauty. Fortunately, Mapperton has its own glory. Folded into an escarpment, the mainly 17th-century house overlooks the garden in the valley below. Octagonal and rectangular pools bustle with large-scale topiary around their edges and, in summer, salvias and dahlias sing out in clarion colours for the benefit of the bird's eye view. Hardy described his version of Wessex as a 'partly real, partly dream country', and the Montagu family, who have lived at Mapperton since the 1950s, have added to the sense of enchantment, with formality loosening towards an arboretum, beyond which the estate is being rewilded, while remaining open for stays and walks.

Mapperton, Beaminster, DT8 3NR
Open March–October
Paid entry
mapperton.com

Hauser & Wirth Somerset

Worth a visit in all seasons

When the Swiss gallerists Ursula Hauser and Iwan and Manuela Wirth opened their free gallery in Somerset in 2014, it raised a few eyebrows – an ambitious undertaking for such an unassuming, tucked-away place. Appointing the Dutch gardening superstar Piet Oudolf, fresh from the High Line in New York City, seemed even more incongruous. Other international outfits have reinvigorated the local landscape since (see The Newt, p.126), but this rectangular enclosure, known as the Oudolf Field, is a gem – and it's easily as big a draw as the gallery. Bounded by a traditional native hedge, its box-like qualities have been elevated with closely planted perennials and spring bulbs, intersected by narrow grass paths. An avenue of pale gravel, studded with mounded grass ovals, has a space-age look, compounded by a giant fibreglass pod on the perimeter (the Radić Pavilion). Plant colour is intense in spring and summer but, as Oudolf said himself, colour is fleeting. More value is put on plant form and resilience, as proved by the field's monochrome display in winter.

Durslade Farm, Dropping Lane, Bruton, BA10 0NL
Open year-round
Free to visit
hauserwirth.com

Caisson Gardens

Inspired land transformation

A new arrival in the canon of classic British gardens, Caisson was made by Phil and Amanda Honey, who have joint experience in landscape design and installing temporary gardens on film sets. This informs the garden's dramatic staging, with pleached crab apples (their branches trained along wires), confident groupings of oversized topiary and an oval pond right outside the front door. At the back, a shady patio sports a double line of white mulberries, put in as mature trees. Wildflowers are everywhere: between paving, in the sloping front lawn (with its picturesque double ribbon of water trickling through), in the walled garden, meadows and woodland. Despite the overall impression, this is a post-industrial site; the Honeys have turned what could have been disadvantages into even more theatre – and biodiversity. A series of deep channels along the drive into the garden and beyond are the remains of waterways and locks built by the Somerset Coal Canal Company. Long since dried out, their presence provided the garden's key: new waterways were created closer to the house, and flora and fauna moved in.

Combe Hay, Bath, BA2 7EF
Open April–June
Paid entry
caissongardens.com

Sezincote

Dares to be different

No photograph can prepare you for the surprise of Sezincote: a mini-Mughal palace facing the rising sun on a Cotswold escarpment. Paintings and aquatints from 200 years ago by the artist Thomas Daniell do a better job of describing the building's domes and minarets, as well as capturing the essence of the garden as it remains today. Sezincote is the result of a collaboration between Regency designers and landowners who made their fortunes trading in the East India Company; it is more homage than pastiche. Guided by venerable trees, views have recently been opened, revealing the 19th-century lake designed by the great designer of the picturesque, Humphry Repton, and a stream that leads down to the double-decker Indian bridge. More recent additions include a Persian garden, designed in the 1950s by the current owner's grandmother. Layers of garden style are kept alive, with expert planting bringing new glamour to island beds. Prepare for more perfection on the drive out through the exquisite village of Bourton-on-the-Hill.

Moreton-in-Marsh, GL56 9AW
Open March–November
Paid entry
sezincote.co.uk

The Newt in Somerset

Splendid pleasure gardens at a luxury hotel

Gardening can seem like a club, forbidding to those who are lacking in hardiness or botanical confidence. The Newt in Somerset understands this hesitation and is run as an accessible members' club of its own, where all levels of knowledge are welcome. Owned by Koos Bekker and Karen Roos, the couple behind the South African vineyard Babylonstoren, the Newt's interest is in cider over wine, and it is the definition of a pleasure garden: eat from the land at one of the top-grade restaurants or cafes (with diverse pricing), then learn about the soil that produced your food. There is little chance of discomfort or mud on this estate; even the 'no-dig' beds in the kitchen garden are immaculate. Cider apple trees are given high status, displayed within the semi-circular walled garden as a maze, trained in arcane and historic ways. The Newt seems to delight in its surroundings, embracing Somerset's folklore and rural tradition through a prism of luxury. Even the local train station of Castle Cary (shared with Glastonbury festival-goers) has had its forecourt revitalised with a functioning creamery, mini-baroque garden and cafe, serving fresh produce from the Newt's market gardens.

Bruton, BA7 7NG
Open year-round
Paid entry (open to members and guests only)
thenewtinsomerset.com

Iford Manor

British eclecticism at its best

The fame of Iford Estate is closely associated with Harold Peto, who bought it in 1899. He became a landscape architect, with the garden as his testing ground. A man of taste and means, he collected artefacts from all over the world, and this house – with its classical facade draped in wisteria and steep terraced gardens – looked a little bit like Italy. He added a loggia (an open-sided gallery), a casita (a separate, smaller house) and Romanesque cloisters for displaying sculptures and friezes in a garden setting. It works because the garden is entirely south-west-facing, with afternoon light perfectly filtered between balcony balustrades and columns entwined with roses. Besides the Italianate quality (plus a mossy Japanese garden), Iford is essentially an Arts and Crafts garden, made more British by its eclecticism; there is even a statue of Britannia standing on the entrance bridge. Visitor numbers are limited for a better experience; well-behaved dogs on leads are welcome, children under 10 are not.

Iford, Bradford-on-Avon, BA15 2BA
Open April–September
Paid entry
ifordmanor.co.uk

Tregrehan Garden

Subtropical collections around a family home

It's easy to drive past the sign for Tregrehan without realising that it's important to stop here. This temperate rainforest includes an ever-growing botanical collection and a fully functioning Victorian glasshouse in the walled garden. Warmed by the Gulf Stream and sheltered on rising ground, Tregrehan was originally planted as an arboretum of rare specimens from around the world. The trees love the conditions: recent records suggest that 280 National Champions – exceptional examples of their species – can be found here, as well as the tallest tree in Cornwall (a Sitka spruce). The same family has owned the estate since 1565 and has been amassing plants for at least 300 years. The line of inheritance has been more fragile than the collection: four generations of heirs have been summoned from New Zealand to take over, including the current proprietor, Tom Hudson. They have often brought plants with them; several champion coniferous and broadleaf trees originated in 19th-century New Zealand, while Hudson continues to add newer Kiwi plant material to the collections of magnolia and camellia species.

Tregrehan House, Par, PL24 2SJ
Open March–October
Paid entry
tregrehangarden.uk

Caerhays Castle & Garden

Laden with prize-winning blooms

Daphne du Maurier's Gothic novel *Rebecca* is partly inspired by Caerhays Castle, with its sandy cove and the presence of rhododendrons in threatening shades of crimson. With Cornwall's mild and damp climate – and the sheltered, sloping and well-drained conditions that the estate provides – all shades of rhododendron thrive here. It's an exotic and dramatic atmosphere (especially when the petals carpet the ground) – a far cry from their more suburban settings in other counties. Caerhays is a private house inhabited by generations of horticultural Williamses, who have bred many prize-winning camellias and daffodils as well as sought-after magnolias (of which Caerhays has the largest National Collection). The castle's privacy is underlined by instructions to park down by the beach and continue your pilgrimage to the grounds on foot. And just as garden visiting gets into gear elsewhere, the gates of this one are firmly closed in June.

Caerhays Estate, Gorran, St Austell, PL26 6LY
Open February–June
Paid entry
visit.caerhays.co.uk

Kiftsgate Court Gardens

Shaped by three generations of women gardeners

With land sloping away steeply in front of the house, canopies of Scots and Monterey pines provide the backdrop to this plantswoman's garden. Or rather three generations of plantswomen; Heather Muir, the grandmother of the current owner, began gardening here in 1920. With encouragement from her friend Lawrence Johnston next door (see Hidcote Manor, p.158), she extended the garden downwards into a series of terraces, built by Italian gardeners in the 1930s. Rock roses mingle with aromatic herbs among the pine needles and the distinctly Mediterranean feel is fitting – she and Johnston were both regulars on the Côte d'Azur. Her daughter, Diany, added a semi-circular swimming pool at the bottom, reflecting the sky and grounding the landscape. *Her* daughter, Anne Chambers, has added the sculptural Water Garden on the top level. Around the house, unusual perennials are masterfully paired with shrubs rather than grasses, while the world-famous Kiftsgate rose causes havoc in the Rose Border, rambling 90 feet along the ground and up three sizeable trees.

Chipping Campden, GL55 6LN
Open April–September
Paid entry
kiftsgate.co.uk

Tremenheere Sculpture Gardens

Even-handed curation of planting and art

Acquired from the monks of St Michael's Mount – a tidal island topped with a medieval castle and chapel – in 1295, the Tremenheere family governed this land for 600 years. The final member to be involved in what is now the sculpture garden would travel down to Cornwall from London by chariot. He had the prescience to plant a native woodland in the 1830s, which helps to shelter subtropical planting in this atmospheric garden. St Michael's Mount makes itself known across the water, aided by a viewing platform among the trees. But the real attraction here is the assured combination of bold structural planting and well-curated art. Dozens of installations and sculptures are scattered along the stream and down the slopes of Tremenheere's 22 acres, and the main draw is *Tewlwolow Kernow* by James Turrell. Its domed interior has an elliptical aperture at the top and an encircling bench below, upon which to sit and gaze up at the ever-changing light. Don't miss the excellent nursery, Surreal Succulents, on the way out.

Near Gulval, Penzance, TR20 8YL

Open February–December

Paid entry

tremenheere.co.uk

Penjerrick Garden

Wonderfully wild garden in South Cornwall

Three sloping Cornish gardens were established by three brothers from a Quaker family in the first decades of the 19th century: Penjerrick, Glendurgan and Trebah. Head to the first one, since it fell on hard times in World War I and, unlike the other two, saw no further development, languishing in a semi-wild state. The brothers collected plants from all over the world – eased by their family shipping business – and tried their luck in the welcoming conditions of temperate, oceanic South Cornwall. Penjerrick is uncompromising towards the comfort of visitors (don't expect to find a WC) and its website coolly advises that by early summer, 'paths get more and more overgrown'. This, of course, is part of the charm; away from Cornwall's crowds, look up in wonder at 16-foot tree ferns (among the first to arrive in the UK) and enjoy the series of ponds in the valley garden down the slope, overhung with giant gunnera (rhubarb).

Budock, Falmouth, TR11 5ED
Open March–September
Paid entry
penjerrickgarden.co.uk

Tresco Abbey Garden

Otherworldly plant paradise

All along the western coasts of the British Isles and Ireland, plants bask in a temperate maritime climate, aided by the warmth of the Gulf Stream. But the Isles of Scilly, southwest of Cornwall, take this to another level, with an early spring, a late autumn and an average winter temperature of 8 degrees Celsius. On the 2-mile-long island of Tresco, Abbey Garden (built around a ruined Benedictine abbey) is a subtropical plant paradise, with resident red squirrels and golden pheasants adding to the otherworldly experience. Leased from the Duchy of Cornwall, the garden was begun in 1834 by Augustus Smith, a horticultural banker from Hertfordshire. He planted Californian trees as a shelter belt and carved out a series of south-facing terraces to accommodate his ever-expanding collection of global plants that thrive in a Mediterranean-like climate zone. Agaves, proteas and tree ferns jostle for space in double borders and along winding pathways; expect to see hundreds of plants in full technicolour, even in midwinter.

Tresco, Isles of Scilly, TR24 0QQ
Open March–October
Paid entry
tresco.co.uk/enjoying/abbey-garden

Coton Manor

Consummate English flower garden, with flamingos

Coton Manor is perhaps the perfect garden visit. Amenities first: the food in the tea room is excellent and the plant nursery is a destination in itself. The 10-acre garden, run by the family who live in the limestone manor (which was razed during the English Civil War and rebuilt shortly after), is a happy scene. Fluffy Barbu d'Uccle chickens wander through the borders and, adding a surreal touch, a small flock of flamingos live by the stream year-round. Masterminded over decades by Susie Pasley-Tyler, there are many seasonal highlights: immaculate hellebores in the woodland garden on view in February before the full opening at Easter; a managed bluebell wood, fragrant and slightly eerie, in April; and fully orchestrated, colour-themed borders that range from cool to hot, separated by wide paths of grass. The feeling at Coton is of an English garden in the grand style, with well-chosen plants that are grown by people who love the place.

Guilsborough, Northampton, NN6 8RQ
Open April–September
Paid entry
cotonmanor.co.uk

Hidcote

The first garden-only gift to the National Trust

The self-effacing entrance to Hidcote Manor, with its simple yard behind painted wooden doors, gives an idea of the original character of the place – and little hint of what it has become: one of the most influential gardens in the world. The first property to be donated to the National Trust for its garden alone, its creator Lawrence Johnston – an American plantsman with an eye for French garden design – got the potential of a Cotswolds farmhouse at the beginning of the 20th century. He divided the 10.5-acre garden into a series of rooms, with colour-coded flower borders that today are full-to-bursting near the house. Further out, hedges become longer and taller, creating a sense of French splendour in this once-working landscape. Contrasts give it energy, and part of Hidcote's genius is in the empty spaces, highlighted by beautifully realised gazebos and gates, extending the view at the end of grassy allées. Avoid the crowds and admire this garden's structure by visiting off-season.

Hidcote Bartrim, near Chipping Campden, GL55 6LR
Open January–November
Paid entry
nationaltrust.org.uk/visit/
gloucestershire-cotswolds/hidcote

Cottesbrooke Hall & Gardens

Glamorous rural pleasure grounds

Rural Northamptonshire lives up to its nickname as the 'county of spires and squires', with untouched villages owned by private estates, in which a horse is never far away. Approaching the hamlet of Cottesbrooke is a journey into the land that time forgot, with narrow gated roads persuading you that the outside world doesn't really exist. Seen across fields, rising above a lake, the 1702 jewel box of Cottesbrooke Hall promises much, and its showcase of a garden delivers even more. There have been contributions from some of Britain's most notable landscape designers over the years, including a masterful terrace by Sir Geoffrey Jellicoe and the tranquil Pool Garden (a former laundry yard) by Dame Sylvia Crowe. Roses are in abundance, as is beautifully clipped yew, while the paving under the Arts and Crafts pergola becomes truly 'crazy'. Privately owned, the aesthetic is as glossy and streamlined as a good steed.

Northampton, NN6 8PF
Open May–September
Paid entry
cottesbrooke.co.uk

Easton Walled Gardens

Middle England's Sleeping Beauty

It's an unusual proposition but it works: an English country garden in which the house no longer exists, having been demolished in the 1950s. Languishing for the rest of the century, the rabbit-infested, bramble-thick landscape sparked the imagination of Lady Ursula Cholmeley, whose husband inherited the land. There are walled enclosures and a few buildings, such as the tantalisingly lovely stable yard and gatehouse, which were spared when the demolition bulldozer ran out of petrol. These, with some graceful steps, balustrades and an ornamental bridge leading to the kitchen garden over the River Witham, are the structural elements that Lady Cholmeley used to create a new landscape. Located off the A1 near Grantham, it is a destination garden, offering a 'pickery' in one of the walled gardens, where visitors can cut sweet peas to buy (and seeds are available from the excellent shop). The larger walled garden is now a sloping meadow, with roses growing over iron supports in the long grass.

Grantham, NG33 5AP
Open year-round
Paid entry
visiteaston.co.uk

The
PICKERY and
FRAME YARD

Trentham Gardens

725 acres near The Potteries

The spectacle of these gardens, with their grand Lake Como feel, seems rather incongruous with their location, just a 10-minute bus ride from Stoke-on-Trent. And yet their respective histories are closely linked. Created by the Dukes of Sutherland, enlisting a who's who of Britain's best landscape designers, Trentham reached its apex in the mid-19th century, with both the house and garden remodelled by Charles Barry (who was also working on the Houses of Parliament). The River Trent, diverted into the mile-long lake, fed the many fountains and ponds in the vast formal garden, but it was polluted by Stoke's potteries, and the whole site was affected. Even when the river was moved again, the great stink remained, and the family left in 1907. Fast-forward to 2004, when the estate began its remarkable comeback. Now a nature reserve in part, the formal areas have been revivified with naturalistic planting from world-class designer Tom Stuart-Smith and Piet Oudolf, while Nigel Dunnett has been restoring the lakeside meadow. His work is aided by beavers, who fell trees, dam areas of water and greatly increase biodiversity.

Stone Road, Trentham, Stoke-on-Trent, ST4 8JG

Open year-round

Paid entry

trentham.co.uk

Doddington Hall & Gardens

Elizabethan manor garden brimming with character

There is so much personality in this gem of a place, partly because it has never been sold or 'cleared out' since 1600, when the building was finished. For admirers of expressive topiary, spreading cedar of Lebanon trees and warm Elizabethan brick walls, the 5-acre garden is a manageable stroll, with longer estate walks leading out into the surrounding countryside. Irises are a speciality here; they are positioned under the west facade of the house, glowing in the afternoon sun. They are expertly managed by Antony Jarvis (whose daughter and family now run the estate); his love of bulbs and rhizomes spreads into the Wild Garden, with well-chosen spring flowers populating the grass around veteran trees. Previous generations preserved the garden's ancient character, savouring the village feel of farm buildings mingling by the house. Cut flowers and food are grown in the walled garden, supplying the outstanding farm shop, cafe and restaurant.

Main Street, Doddington, Lincoln, LN6 4RU
Open February–September
Paid entry
doddingtonhall.com

Lowther Castle & Gardens

Outstanding revival of a lost garden

Built in the early 19th century as a 'sham castle', Lowther is now an actual ruin, and a marvellous setting for imaginative garden design. The 7th Earl of Lonsdale, a farmer, tried and failed to give away the crumbling pile in the 1950s, and had to make do by using the garden for chickens, pigs and timber. On removing the roof of the building but leaving the facade and outer walls, he inadvertently created romance with some lovely ruins. Today, his grandson, Jim Lowther, is in the process of rewilding the estate, elevating the garden in collaboration with the revered designer, Dan Pearson. The Rose Garden is now an interpretation of *Sleeping Beauty*, encircled by briar roses, with inner beds shaped as petals. The main triumphs are around the remaining castle walls: the forecourt's Tapestry Garden has angular asymmetrical beds that are blurred over the season by grasses and perennials and the Garden-in-the-Ruins makes the most of the castle remains, with high walls and window arches curtained by vines and exotic climbers.

Lowther, Penrith CA10 2HH
Open year-round
Paid entry
lowthercastle.org

Hepworth Wakefield Garden

Open-air gallery that never closes

Be prepared to leave the car in a nearby retail park: the Hepworth is slotted into an industrial part of Wakefield and its immediate space is devoted to people and plants rather than parking. When Tom Stuart-Smith won a competition to attract visitors to the gallery by way of the garden, he responded to the angular volumes of the David Chipperfield building with his own angled beds. Some of them are home to sculptures that rise out of prairie planting in a similar manner to the trees around the periphery. Pieces of hedging bend around corners instead of enclosing beds entirely; in autumn, the changing colours of clipped beech complement blackening seed heads and undaunted grasses. In spring, crab apples blossom around a tulip display that honours Wakefield's history of cultivating the flower since 1836. Open to all, day and night, the garden is an easy cut-through, but mainly it's a place to stop and return to over the seasons.

Tootal Street, Wakefield, WF1 5AW
Open year-round
Free to visit (garden only)
hepworthwakefield.org

The Alnwick Garden

Ambitious design on a grand scale

Alnwick is firmly associated with the current Duchess of Northumberland, who saw a blank slate around her castle and resolved to make it the most magnificent new garden in Europe. It certainly holds a few records on the world stage: the biggest tree house (containing a restaurant), play structure and collection of Tai Haku cherry trees (with 329 trees dropping their white petals at once). She also has the UK's 'deadliest' poison garden, a collection of toxic, intoxicating and narcotic plants, only open to guided tours. Among the beautifully designed flame-shaped beds are familiar garden plants like hellebore and laurel – these too can kill you. Elsewhere, a water cascade lined with domed hornbeam (and windows) reflects the scale of Alnwick's ambition; on moving into the castle 30 years ago, the Duchess enlisted the help of landscape architect Jacques Wirtz, who had recently renovated the garden at Élysée Palace, the French presidential residency. Alnwick is on one of the UK's most scenic coastline bus routes; catch the X18 from Newcastle or Berwick.

Denwick Lane, Alnwick, NE66 1FJ
Open year-round
Paid entry
alnwickgarden.com

Chatsworth

Quintessential stately home and grounds

There is an enjoyable swagger to Chatsworth, making it a worthwhile destination for a longer visit. Splendidly placed against an enfolding scene of wooded hills in the Derbyshire Dales, the approach reveals a palace with gold-framed windows glinting in the afternoon, sheep strolling through the Capability Brown park and a bridge over the River Derwent. Attractions have been added and subtracted over the centuries: the remaining foundations of a vast conservatory, built by the 6th Duke of Devonshire's gardener-turned-engineer Joseph Paxton and demolished after World War I, now contain a yew maze. Set pieces include the Cascade, a Baroque water feature that tumbles down the lawn behind the house, and Paxton's great water jet (called the Emperor Fountain) to one side. Mature conifers tower over the garden's edges. Much plant matter has been added this century, from star names such as Tom Stuart-Smith and Dan Pearson, but gardeners, like dukes, come and go, yet Chatsworth sails on regardless. Make sure to stay in one of the satellite villages, which seem built for hospitality; the experience is best described in *Pride and Prejudice*.

Bakewell, DE45 1PP
Open March–January
Paid entry
chatsworth.org

Dove Cottage

Restored garden from the Romantic Era

Although there are numerous 'Wordsworth lived here' sites around Grasmere, Dove Cottage (now rebranded as Wordsworth Grasmere) is the most evocative of the poet and his sister Dorothy, a diarist. Behind the small roadside house, Wordsworth's 'domestic slip of mountain' still holds an informally arranged garden with an orchard, where the siblings would rest and write. They also retreated to their Moss Hut at the top of the site, a shelter with views. Gardening cheaply, they planted wildflowers that they gathered on walks, such as columbine, white foxgloves and thyme. Cottage life was enlivened by extended visits from poets and writers, and when the Wordsworths moved out, Thomas de Quincey moved in – and wrote about taking opium in the study. He also took an axe to the beloved garden, cutting down shrubs and destroying the little hut. Thankfully, the cottage was bought by the Wordsworth Trust in 1890, and further vandalism was prevented. Today, the Garden Orchard retains an unassuming air, with recent investment restoring its nature-based spirit, and a new Moss Hut.

Grasmere, Ambleside, LA22 9PP

Open year-round

Paid entry

wordsworth.org.uk

RHS Garden Bridgewater

Expertise and designer panache

If you live near one of the Royal Horticultural Society's five main public gardens, count yourself lucky; if you are travelling near one, make a detour. A superior plant nursery and bookshop are guaranteed, but the landscapes are distinguished too, backed by the research and expertise on which the RHS prides itself. Bridgewater, its latest public garden, is a former country estate next to Salford, and both have seen a revival in the last 15 years. The scale of ongoing restoration is impressive; the Weston Walled Garden alone covers 11 acres. Paradise Garden, the bigger walled enclosure, has been given a cool elegance by Tom Stuart-Smith, with rills (small streams), fountains and beds containing 27,000 plants. The Kitchen Garden, with elaborately espaliered fruit trees on the old walls, incorporates herbal and forest areas with high-spec detail throughout, care of young designers Harris Bugg. Do not expect pastiche in the Chinese Streamside Garden, which has been developed with the local Chinese community; do expect a programme of old-fashioned flower shows from venerable plant societies.

Worsley, Salford, M28 2LJ

Open year-round

Paid entry

rhs.org.uk/gardens/bridgewater

Dilston Physic Garden

An un-grand botanic attraction

The healing properties of plants are well-documented, but not always well broadcast. If you've ever wondered about the link between hedgerow plants and the pills offered in health food shops, you're not alone; the Dilston Physic Garden was founded on exploring this connection. Established in the 1990s, this immensely calming two-acre garden has developed slowly to restore habitat and biodiversity, as well as the human spirit. Take time to learn about traditional land practices, developed by people over millennia (and only neglected in the last century), such as coppicing willow; laying hedges with health-giving elderberry, hawthorn and wild rose; and managing woodlands and orchards with their attendant wildflowers. Seven hundred varieties of healing plants are grown here for the benefit of humans and other fauna. Arrive by foot; Dilston is a 20-minute walk along the road from Corbridge train station or a scenic walk along the River Tyne via the Corbridge Heritage Trail.

Corbridge, NE45 5QZ
Open March–December
Paid entry
dilstonphysicgarden.com

BURDOCK
Arctium lappa

Nant-y-Bedd

A garden in the forest

It's only ten miles from the accommodating town of Abergavenny, but Nant-y-Bedd (meaning 'Stream of the Grave') is a world away – high up in the Brecon Beacons and almost hidden at the end of a five-mile lane, where satellite navigation technology is useless. Plan, consult the informative website for directions and pre-book. A cottage garden behind a prim picket fence announces that here, in the middle of a Norway spruce plantation, lies something special. The stone cottage is the home of avid gardener and communicator Sue Mabberley and her husband, Ian, for whom this organic garden, wrested from the woodland, is their life's work. Over the stream from the front garden, wildflowers mix with vegetables in an informal potager, climbing over hazel supports. Beyond this, a rope bridge over a gorge leads to wilder meadow areas, featuring a natural swimming pond and a two-storey tree house, straddling a stout sycamore.

Forest Coal Pit, Abergavenny, NP7 7LY
Open in summer; check dates via website
Paid entry
nantybedd.com

Plas Brondanw Gardens

Where the landscape is the star of the show

The idea of a 'borrowed landscape' – incorporating background scenery into garden design – is used to great effect here. With its views over Snowdonia National Park (Eryri), the architect Clough Williams-Ellis's home garden is generally considered to be lovelier than his more famous creation, Portmeirion Village. On inheriting the 500-year-old house at Plas Brondanw in his mid-twenties (in 1908), Williams-Ellis took the Italian Renaissance as his inspiration, making radial axes through the garden that guide the eye towards the drama of the scenery. Pyramid-shaped Cnicht Mountain is framed at the end of a path by a turquoise gate (the estate's trademark shade, used on all the metalwork). Outsized topiary is deployed in a scale appropriate to the tall house, and velvety lawns are edged by borders that are more green and shrubby than flower-filled. The wonderful cafe (open seasonally from March to October) is a draw, as is the gallery inside the house. For climbers, a false ruin at the top of a woodland walk provides 360-degree views of Snowdonia.

Llanfrothen, Penrhyndeudraeth, LL48 6SW
Open year-round
Paid entry
cloughwilliamsellis.org/Garden

Plas yn Rhiw

Rescued landscape by the sea

When three sisters came to look at the small, derelict manor at Plas yn Rhiw in 1938, the garden was so overgrown that they had to climb through a window to get in. They were mainly interested in the ancient woodland that came with the house, having long admired the view from across Hell's Mouth Bay. They slowly restored the sheltered, sea-facing garden, revealing paths and box hedging under brambles. The siblings sourced plants that benefitted from the microclimate, including a still-thriving Himalayan Magnolia tree, planted in 1946. They purchased land that had been sold from the estate piecemeal, and formed a plan early on to preserve it via the National Trust. When the last sister died in 1981, strict instructions were left, forbidding the use of 'poisonous sprays and preparations', which could harm colonies of Welsh black honeybees that still live in the roof. An orchard of locally native fruit trees is a recent addition to the Trust's only organic garden in Wales.

Rhiw, Pwllheli, Gwynedd, LL53 8AB
Open March–October
Paid entry
nationaltrust.org.uk/visit/wales/plas-yn-rhiw

The Fife Arms

Charmed landscape with hospitality

If your idea of the Highlands is a Scots Baronial vision of tartans and stone crenellations, the Fife Arms fulfils that and more. Fifteen minutes from Balmoral, this large riverside hostelry was rebooted in 2019 by Hauser & Wirth (p.114). Although everything about it says 'luxury experience', the public bar remains true to its name: open to all. The Flying Stag, serving reasonably priced haggis, neeps and tatties, offers easy access to the garden, designed by esteemed landscape gardener Jinny Blom. Rearranged over two levels with the help of rocky banks and engineered steps, Blom created a sense of enchantment out of a junk-filled yard, using intrinsically Scottish trees such as rowan (said to keep away evil spirits) and shrubs such as Scotch rose and bog myrtle (said to repel midges). Refined azaleas and red hot pokers evoke Victorian tastes with contemporary panache, lit with acid yellow grasses. Conceived as 'a fairy woodland', the garden merges into wider views of the Cairngorms beyond.

Mar Road, Braemar, Ballater, AB35 5YN
Open year-round
Free entry via The Flying Stag
thefifearms.com

Ardkinglas Woodland Garden

Nature and nurture in the West Highlands

The scenery of Argyll is famously breathtaking, with unpeopled beaches, crystalline waters and an almost midnight sun in midsummer. Sometimes, though, it feels essential to embrace some human landscapes, to see whether it is possible to enhance what is already beautiful. Ardkinglas is a 14th-century estate founded by the Campbell clan; later owners planted a pinetum (an arboretum for conifers) in 1875. Bathed by the Gulf Stream's warming vapours and a receptive acid soil, impressive pines, firs and spruces from around the world have grown remarkably tall and wide. One of the champion trees here is a silver fir, the 'mightiest conifer in Europe' (noted by the 10th Duke of Argyll). Beyond the majestic trees, this is a relaxed garden, with drama added in May and June by bluebells spreading around rhododendrons and budding azaleas. Across the shore of Loch Fyne, Inveraray Castle is another Campbell stronghold and strikes a contrasting note, with historic formal gardens designed to flatter the grandeur of the house.

Ardkinglas Estate, Cairndow, PA26 8BG

Open year-round

Paid entry

ardkinglas.com

Little Sparta

Ian Hamilton Finlay's garden of 'physical' poems

'Certain gardens are described as retreats when they are really attacks,' wrote the poet and artist Ian Hamilton Finlay. His point is realised all over Little Sparta, not least in a pair of classical gate posts topped with giant stone hand grenades. Visitors to these five acres of former farmland in the Pentland Hills should not expect to be rewarded with a cup of tea in a sculpture garden; there are no refreshments on offer, and the whole garden is a work of art. With the help of his wife, Sue, Finlay began the garden in the 1960s as a setting for 'physical' poems, puns and aphorisms. Over the years, he was able to afford skilled stone masons and letter carvers, but the garden came about slowly, with Finlay planting trees and digging ponds, and Sue 'tending the poems'. Themes range around modern warfare, the French Revolution and ancient Rome, but equally, sailing and rural nostalgia – experienced in the context of changing light and weather.

Stonypath, Dunsyre, ML11 8NG
Open June–September
Paid entry
littlesparta.org.uk

CUMULUS·STRATUS·CUMULO

THE
IS
OF
SAINT

JUST
FUTURE

Picture credits:

p.2 Caisson Gardens © Jason Ingram; p.4 Plas yn Rhiw © The National Trust Photolibrary; p.5 Great Dixter © Kay Roxby; p.6 Charleston © Lee Robins; Chelsea Physic Garden first and second image © Sam Bush, third image © Marco Kesseler; Barbican Estate first image © Taran Wilkhu, second image © Claire Takacs; The Garden Museum © Eve Nemeth; Kew Gardens first image © Marco Kesseler, second image © Daniel Berehulak; OmVed Gardens first image, © Will Hearle, second image © Thomas Broadhead, third & fourth images © OmVed; Inner Temple Garden first image © Claire Takacs, following images © Richard Bloom; Horniman Museum Gardens first image © Jooney Woodward, second image © Richard Bloom; Covent Garden Playground & Gardens © Covent Garden Playground & Gardens; The Regent's Park first image © PhotoLondonUK, second image © Ellen Rooney; The Exchange © Richard Bloom; Eden Nature Garden © Jooney Woodward; Kelmscott Manor first image © Britt Willoughby Dyer, second image © Society of Antiquaries of London (Kelmscott Manor); Sissinghurst © Jason Ingram; Cotswold Wildlife Park & Gardens first image © Skowron, following images © Britt Willoughby Dyer; Rousham House & Gardens © Britt Willoughby Dyer; Great Dixter © Richard Bloom; Magdalen College Gardens © Andrew Lawson; Benton End © Ngoc Minh Ngo; Prospect Cottage © Carolyn Clark; Waltham Place © Niki McCann / Waltham Place; Balmoral Cottage © Carole Drake; The World Garden, Lullingstone Castle © Stephen Sangster; Charleston first image © Hollie Fernando, second image © Emma Croman, third image Marco Kesseler, fourth image © Lewis Ronald; Ventnor Botanic Garden first image © Julian Winslow, second image © Ventnor Botanic Garden, third image © Ian Dagnall, fourth image © Adam Gasson; Cambridge Botanic Garden first image © Geoffrey Robinson, second image © David Bartlett; Newnham College Gardens © Will Pryce; Houghton Hall & Gardens first image © SPK, second image Claudio Parmiggiani, Axis of the World, third image Richard Long, Houghton Cross, fourth image Richard Long, Full Moon Circle, images 2–4 © Houghton Hall, photo by Pete Huggins; The Manor at Hemingford Grey © Marianne Majerus; Pensthorpe © Richard Bloom; Mapperton © Andrew Montgomery; Hauser & Wirth Somerset © Richard Bloom; Cassion Gardens © Jason Ingram; Sezincote © Britt Willoughby Dyer; The Newt in Somerset © The Newt in Somerset; Iford Manor first image © Iford Manor, second image © Clive Nichols; Tregrehan Garden © Alex Ramsay; Caerhays Castle & Garden first image © Peter Schickert, second image © Clive Nichols; Kiftsgate Court Gardens © Sabina Ruber; Tremenheere Sculpture Gardens © Karl Davies; Penjerrick Garden © Gordon Scammell; Tresco Abbey Garden first image © James Osmond, second image © Rob Besant; Coton Manor first image © Photoimageon, following images © Kendra Wilson; Hidcote © Britt Willoughby Dyer; Cottesbrooke Hall & Gardens © Clive Nichols; Easton Walled Gardens first image © Steffie Shields, following images © Jim Monk; Trentham Gardens first image © Dean Nixon, second image © Jon D; Doddington Hall & Gardens © Christopher Chambers; Lowther Castle & Gardens © Ngoc Minh Ngo; Hepworth Wakefield Garden © Jason Ingram; The Alnwick Garden first image © Jiri Vondrous, second image © Amitav Ghosh, third image © Michael Brooks; Chatsworth first image © David Chapman, second image © Jason Ingram; Dove Cottage © Gareth Gardner for Nissen Richards Studio; RHS Garden Bridgewater © Jason Ingram; Dilston Physic Garden © David Taylor; Nant-y-Bedd © Jason Ingram; Plas Brondanw Gardens © Richard Bloom; Plas yn Rhiw © The National Trust Photolibrary; The Fife Arms © Britt Willoughby Dyer; Ardkinglas Woodland Garden first and third image © David Collins, second image © Jack Hobhouse, fourth image © imageBroker; Little Sparta first image © Robin Gillanders, second image © Gardenpics.

Britain's Best Gardens
First edition, first printing

First published in 2026 by Hoxton Mini Press, London.
Copyright © Hoxton Mini Press 2026. All rights reserved.
Text © Kendra Wilson 2026

Text by Kendra Wilson
Front cover illustration by Sean Thomas
Editing by Florence Ward
Series design by Hoxton Mini Press
Production design by Dom Grant
Production control by David Brimble
Proofreading by Kate Overy
Editorial support by Richard Enright

A CIP catalogue record for this book is available from the British Library.
The right of Kendra Wilson to be identified as the author of this Work has
been asserted under the Copyright, Designs and Patents Act 1988.

ISBN: 978-1-917719-13-1

Printed and bound by Balto Print, Lithuania

Manufacturer: Hoxton Mini Press, 104 Northside Studios,
16–29 Andrews Road, London E8 4QF, UK. www.hoxtonminipress.com

Represented by: Authorised Rep Compliance Ltd., Ground Floor,
71 Lower Baggot Street, Dublin D02 P593, Ireland. www.arccompliance.com

Hoxton Mini Press is an environmentally conscious publisher, committed
to offsetting our carbon footprint. This book is 100 per cent carbon
compensated, with offset purchased from Stand For Trees.

Every time you order from our website, we plant a tree: www.hoxtonminipress.com

KENDRA WILSON

Kendra Wilson began garden writing when she moved to the country, after working as a journalist in London and New York. On visiting a historic garden in Northamptonshire, she began volunteering (and then training) as a gardener who couldn't stop reporting. She now lives in Oxford.

HOXTON MINI PRESS

Hoxton Mini Press is a small indie publisher based in east London. We are committed to making beautiful but affordable books that don't screw up the planet. We offset all our printing, and we hope that the trees we do use will continue their life as books that you'll pass on to your grandchildren.